ROOTS
BRAND
AND
IMAGE

Shivani Gohil

RIGI PUBLICATION

ROOTS BRAND AND IMAGE

By

Shivani Gohil

Originally published in India

ISBN: 978-93-88393-40-9 (Paperback)
978-93-88393-41-6 (eBook)

Published by RIGI PUBLICATION

777, Street no.9, Krishna Nagar Khanna-141401 (Punjab), India

Website: www.rigipublication.com

Email: info@rigipublication.com

Phone: +91-9357710014, +91-9465468291

Preface

The aim of one's life should be to strengthen their roots with full potential so as to lead life with a step ahead.

When we arrive at the word 'Brand' immediately many title strikes ones' mind i.e.; Reebok, Titan, Google, Amazon, Microsoft, etc. But have 'YOU' ever imagined yourself as a 'Brand'?

This book will make you travel through the unique concept of identifying and creating yourself as a unique brand highlighting you in the mob wherever you are! Great leader of 20th century, Father of the Nation, Mahatma Gandhi, who got India its freedom, and also paved the way for South Africa's movement against apartheid, Sound of aeroplane that reminds us of Wright Brothers who proved that man could fly, the super hero Amitabh Bachchan and many more presents a sort of unique brand in their area of workings and what about the general public? Have you ever thought of becoming the brand and create an image different from others that represent 'YOU'?

All this people have walked into the unexplored and undefined path and strived to be unique. Well, this book will reveal the perfect image that one need to create to lead their wish corner in their life. You need to focus on the things that you need to create and begin to implement them in a proper way. Everyone wants to earn money, doing some sort of work sitting behind gadgets hiding themselves from the Real You! But to lead the time your right kind of image pays you first.

"REMEMBER IMAGE CAN CREATE YOU, IMAGE

CAN DISMANTLE YOU"

Presenting your relevant details whether personal or professional to outside world is important to lead your current situation. It will take no time to destroy your image. Every youth wants to be unique, that is, YOU! But the world around you is doing its best, to make you just everybody else. The challenge is to never stop fighting until you arrive at your defined position and generate the strong roots that build you from inside out.

'You have to decide whether you want to be a UNIQUE YOU or Everybody else?'

ASK YOURSELF-

WHAT I WILL BE REMEMBERED FOR?

I would like you to think about what is going to make you unique from others. Be your own brand and create your own image. Make your personality roar your presence, know the brand within you!

If you are given a blank canvas what you will do to create your unique image? Well;

"how to fill the blank canvas with the unique colors that you want to fill in your personality to make it influential is in your hands!

Let's see how this book is going to help you to bring your inside-out.

YOU HAVE TO DECIDE WHETHER YOU WANT TO READ THE TITLE OR OPEN THE BOOK AND INCULCATE THE CHANGE WITHIN YOU!

Shivani Gohil

CONTENTS

ROOTS- BRAND AND IMAGE

**"Construct strong roots called your Brand and Image,
If Roots are strong, no one can make you turn
Undefined!"**

[1]
CREATE YOUR OWN UNIQUE CREATION

'IMAGE SPEAKS'

Wouldn't it be wonderful to have people wanting to be around you because they recognize you as a person of quality? What about exceptional women who stands out in the crowd? Having considered every aspect together; image and good reputation goes a long way towards getting you noticed, known and remembered for all the right reasons. Wherever you go, wherever you have to get presented; you should always carry yourself in an authentic manner. You should be unique in the crowd to carry a special attention towards you in an appropriate manner.

Make sure that everything you wear so and say demonstrates that you are a person of high quality and integrity and everything you select for you send a congruent, correct and reasonable message.

What makes your image?

- Your character defined and projected to the public.
- A unique representation of yourself.
- An expressive representation.

- Creation of mental picture.
- Projected image of what you want to show to public and how others perceive you are.

By pretending to be someone other than who we really are, we dishonor ourselves and rob others of the chance to get to know us. By hiding our true-selves, we disrespect our-selves, which further diminish self-esteem as well as confidence. The word "I" is sufficient to define 'yourself'. Always carry yourself with positive and correct affirmations.

While assessing image of any person; whole person shall be looked into. Like for instance; who she is, what she represents, the role she plays in her life, such as wife, mother, daughter, single and dating, career women or volunteer while creating your image and brand. Your character, intelligence, likeability, charm, personal perspective, communication and many other aspects are to be considered.

Everyone knows reel can't be real; show your real self to others. This will make you the cornerstone to develop your personal brand. Don't just run behind the brand that will be put on by you in the form of clothing, accessories or whatnot! But in addition to this, create 'You' as a brand because everybody else is taken. Your inside-out will make you brand rather than leading a common man's life; while other outside brand are everlasting, you can put them anytime you want to. Become foundation of an image that can be proud of one that will honor your authentic self and communicate in to the rest of the world.

Remember, you are always communicating to outside world in one form or other. Whether you say the words or don't say you are still communicating. Even a small child, who cannot speak, showcases his sayings through his postures and gestures which results in communication. Everything about the way you look, the way you walk, the way you attend people sends message to other about what your value is. Your body position, facial expression, your posture, and energy everything speaks about you.

If you want to be successful and want to have people take you seriously, discover what your image is silently telling others.

Remember-

- Importance of your first impression.
- Connection with audience.
- Being appropriate for environment, relationships, clients or any kind of event.
- Reflect best aspects of your personality, your life, your career, your business, your service, your profession.
- Being ethical.
- Self-analysis.
- Presenting best of you.
- Creating your uniqueness so that you get noticed, known and remembered.

All this leads you towards the creation of you apart from others.

***

[2]
PERSONAL BRANDING

‘KNOW THE BRAND WITHIN YOU’

‘BRAND…?’*Oh yes*, as this word strikes our head we think of great brands that exists around us and we always strive to get that brands with us or over us. But have you ever thought that you can also be the brand. Yes, am talking about identifying yourselves as a brand to make ones inside-out! Inside-out is nothing but identifying your inside qualities that will help you put outside as a unique brand. As I talk about the word brand, everyone has a lot to say about it. Let’s talk taking an example, say any famous personality that strikes your mind first, you start thinking about them and can tell many great works or services provided by them and they are known for! *But, what about you?* You are the one who never thought to become a brand and lead a simple life as the general public is leading. Have you ever thought, what people might be gossiping at you when you leave a particular place? Or what kind of impression you are creating on people at a place you visit? How you influence others in terms of your work, your attire, your grooming, your clothing selection, your communication, your appearance, important etiquettes and a lot more. Identifying your personal brand will make you stand as a different ‘you’ in thousands of people. Well, this is not just telling you people to have a change within you stressing on these factors but it involves a process to be a brand that help you identify your potential for the value offering by you (it needs a proper consulting for making you identify your inside-out). Personal branding implies to everyone in the world which is considered very important nowadays. As this term *Personal Branding* is not a concise concept but involves a process to go through for developing a real uniqueness in you and so it applies differently for different people, then maybe you are in service sector, business sector, an actor, businessman, entrepreneur, housewife or any individual. Just sitting behind electronic devices one thinks that they are hiding their-selves from contacts with the people or attending them but the fact is they are creating a *minus skill* to their worth personality or must say a bad impression!!

Again taking an example,

Unlike some other professionals/ professions where the basic foundation of required skills does not change over the time, digital marketing is constantly evolving space. Need of skilled and creative people in the field remains unchanged, changing trends mean that methods and processes utilized can change quickly. If you do not keep yourself updated on the latest industrial development you are likely to be replaced by someone else more suited for. You can keep yourself updated on the latest about digital marketing through online resources, blogs, and write-ups.

Building relationships is also one of the important factors to get emphasized on. Knowing the right people can make a huge difference, so it is important to reach out and build relationships to create a robust network on popular platforms.

'Personal branding adds bonus to your presentation and outlook.'

Let me ask you an easy question, "Do you believe in yourself? Do you accept yourself the way you are, the way you are made because that is what is going to take you establish your identity, that is what will able to build your personal brand because you need to accept the way you are!

What is your Personal Brand? Whether it is the combination of your strengths, your passions, your values, your purpose that you bring and I want you to go on journey of discovering yourself.

'Move out of your comfort zone, work on courage zone.'

***

[3]
AUTHENTIC YOU

'GET TO THE TITLE THAT DEFINES YOU!!'

How many times have you looked into the mirror and thought: *"if I could change or replace this or that part of the body, then only I would have looked a beauty and be pleased with the way I look?"* Majority of people live with this dissatisfaction. If you really want to come out of this, enhance yourself and try to project your best and relevant image. Accept the way you are!

There is powerful connection between you, your brain, your soul and the way you look and feel. Just looking good or feeling good is not enough to project your image rather it comes from your body talk, self-talk, beliefs, habits. Once you start loving your body, automatically self-confidence will boost and you will start feeling energetic and happy. You should know how to create a new beauty trend and perform your own fashion statement. You don't need someone's opinion, to accept the reality. Taking care of yourself from inside helps you enhance and improve your outside. Make yourself comfortable and authentic by-

- Great smile and laughs
- Think gorgeous
- Dare to dance

- Breath in open air
- Be confident
- Buy first class and top quality always
- Have special time for own
- Be different
- Conceal your imperfections
- Don't forget to love yourself

Well, concentrate to create authentic you. If you won't then who will?

"You Don't Need Someone's Opinion to Accept the Reality"

***

[4]
IDENTIFYING YOUR VALUE OFFERING

Your personality is truly influencing factor and allows you to stand in the series of sequence. *'Be yourself, because everyone else is taken.'*

Just because you are sitting behind laptop or mobile phones doesn't mean you have ability to share your personality with the world.

'HUMANS CONNECT WITH HUMANS AND NOT WITH LOGO'S!!'

Considering an activity below,

Suppose you are having any product to sale into market. What will you do? You'll highlight your product to come up and you behind it!

Personal branding helps you to highlight yourself differently as if may be you are an employee, student, entrepreneur, or in any working field.

What you have to do is identifying your value offering.

Well, for understanding this we have value balance scale. Each of the buckets represents unique value offerings.

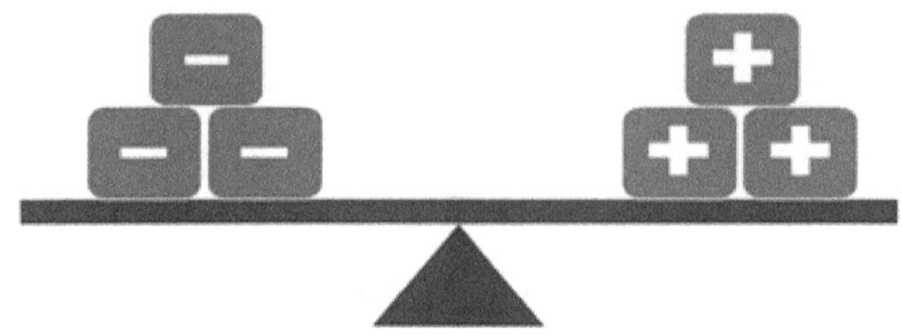

I suggest you to select any six areas of your content as per importance.

There are six buckets that define you-

- Education
- Entertainment
- Inspiration
- Communication
- Information
- Reciprocation

All this should be balanced; anything missing from it may off balance your scale and strategy. I can stress on reciprocation. It is huge value you can offer to your audience. Always remember, *'may the next few months of your life be a period of magnificent transformations.'*

***

[5]
ATTITUDE, VALUES AND ETHICS

ATTITUDE

Your attitude reflects your position. Attitude reflects your likes, dislikes, choices for an item. It can be positive, negative or neutral. Attitude drives behavior. By choosing our attitude whether positive or negative we indulge ourselves in that mood and create respective environment around. This impacts not only us but to others as well.

We should ask ourselves, "What kind of Attitude to adopt?" There's nothing in any situation that tells us we must react one way or other. People who maintain positive attitude are significantly less likely to show signs of aging and more likely to become stronger and healthier than those who possess negative attitude.

Tips to develop positive attitude-

- Choose to be happy
- Give positive instructions to yourself
- Learn to master your thoughts
- Think and visualize only what you want to get happen
- Concentration and meditation is must

- Look at bright side of life
- Read inspiring quotes or blogs
- Keep motivating yourself
- Find reasons to smile

The right thinking and your approach as attitude in correct way will lead you towards positive results.

For developing a correct attitude, firstly; one must choose the attitude you want to develop. Secondly; set goal for making change in your thoughts and identifying the problems to give you a right sense of solution for the same. Thirdly; journalize means journalizing the things so that you get a proper determination for the work and for yourself hoe things have gone so far. Fourth is visualizing means to relax and visualize yourself doing some things that illustrates your new attitude. For example if you want to look more confident see yourself as if you are confident enough and you can see in the person's eye. Visualization will help you to stimulate growth and is refer as to change in attitude. Fifth; 21 days formula, change require time and it takes 21 days working on specific area to inculcate change within you. Also, resolve now to spend time on attitude changes throughout your life. Removing wrong attitude on a regular basis makes room for the right attitude to flourish. Sixth is self-talking; compliment yourself to have positive approach, to work best. Seventh; provide affirmations, put your right-ups affirming that "I am fit and healthy, I am successful, I am patient, etc. these affirmations will help your unconscious believes to work and make to make that come true. Eighth is acting as if; act as if you are the person what you want to be and what you have imagined yourself as. Acting as if may seem difficult the first time you do it, but like anything else, the more you act as if, the better you become.

VALUES

Values are for making choices based on the ideas what is right and what is wrong? They are the choices that we make. They are through life and gained experiences that we develop. We give expression to our values by the choices we make. Core values are the same throughout lives whereas some evolve through lifetime, through personal growth, through career development as and when we experience subject to change. As we grow up and develop, each source of influence contributes to our definition of what is important of life.

Values are the basis which applies to oneself or many. There are different values which work with change in surrounding in which we are present.

- *Personal Values –*
  Personal values are the one which applies to an individual in which he is during a particular time. It evolves from situations with external world and is changeable from time to time. These may derive from particular groups or culture or religion etc. Personal values are not universal but are derived from one's family, generation or whatever the case maybe.
  Every individual possess a unique quality, knowledge, experience, feelings that results into their personal values. So, what are your personal values? Know your personal values and see how you are expressing them outside.

- *Cultural Values –*
  Working in society or groups with different values put together by sharing and identifying knowledge, characteristics, situations, conditions that people of the society considers important are valuable. Cultural values are the values of society and one must know how to get applied to them.

Wearing white clothing and appearing solemn are normative behaviors at a funeral. They reflect the values of respect and support of friends and family.

- *Corporate Values –*
  Corporate values are first order values used and inculcated at corporate culture. These values tells us getting close to customers, but are derived from the fundamentals inside and outside the organization. Apart from only making money there are visionary ideology that constitutes good for people, good for society.

"It is important to know that best builders are constantly building in every field and improving their networks, and you should do the same!!!"

ETHICS

Ethics seeks to raise and address questions based upon morality that speaks about what is good and bad, right and wrong, justice and virtue, and the list not stops.

While working with business ethics you must know principles and ethical problems faced in business environment, if you know them properly they will help you to survive in the competition. It applies to all aspects of business conduct and is relevant to the conduct of individuals and business organizations as a whole. Ethics tells what humans ought to do in terms of obligations, right, benefits to society plus includes honesty, compassion and loyalty.

Business Ethics –

Gearing yourself for the business, business ethics is important pillar during your training period. Considering the below factors will help you out with your prospect.

- Confidentiality –
  Be confidential with your business information. As a trainee working during your work tenure, you may be exposed to the most confidential data of your client's business operation. It's your foremost responsibility to respect the confidentiality and not to share it with family and friends. Leakage of confidential business information may have serious implications in future. So, always carry respect for confidential information of your own organization that comes to your knowledge.

- Independence –
  While working with a client with whom you have any personal relations or with whom you have financial interests, it is preferable that you may inform your senior about the same so that you are not assigned the work of that client.
  In case, if you are assigned with the same, you must ensure that your professional responsibilities shall not in any way affect by your personal interests / relations and you should maintain your objective to be fulfilled along with your independence.

- Do not accept gifts or favors from clients-
  Most of the times, you may come across situation where you may be offered with gifts or favors from clients. But being a professional you must hold dignity in the highest esteem. Good professional ethics demand that you should never accept any personal favors from clients.

- Honesty-
  Be honest with your seniors. Hiding any mistake or not disclosing any fact may cause any serious implications. Where any fact has come to your knowledge or any mistake has occurred, you must disclose it with your senior so that appropriate action can be taken to rectify the same.

***

[6]
IMAGE CREATION OF 'YOU'

As an Image Consultant and Corporate Trainer, it is always said-

'When passion for style meets passion for building people, image consultant is born.'

Image of person makes him stand in the race of winning. Your image is as important as your services you provide. It tells *"What makes you different?"* well, from everyone. If you are exactly the same as next guy it's going to be hard to develop a meaningful brand or an image of yours. The good news is, hardly anyone is exactly the same as the next guy. You have strength, beliefs, ideas that make you realize your differences and what makes you unique from anyone else.

Focus on your competitive advantage, and when it comes to building a brand remember to celebrate your differences as well.

Ask yourself-

- What makes me great?
- What makes me compelling?
- What makes me unique?
- What creates people to take interest, attention, admiration in me?

Branding is your reputation. Branding is about building a name for yourself, showcasing what sets you apart from others, and describing the added value you bring to a situation.

For creating an image which is much focal with the services you provide or work in, it is important to consider following factors. These are the main factors to be considered in human being as people seem to forget to use this to work in their lives.

Talking about the factors will tell you how important they are to remember because best brand builders are constantly building and improving their networks, and you should do the same to make you stand in today's world. Sometimes creating image seems like personality development also but, image consulting provides nutshell to Personality development.

Let's consider the factors-

- Nutrition and communication
- Public speaking
- Fashion marketing
- Understanding the different cultures
- Marketing and networking
- Poor first impression
- Speech help
- Lack of style
- Right kind of Grooming needed in the area of working
- Hate shopping
- Knowledge in identifying the texture of clothes to be suited to your skin
- Color identification
- Lack of self confidence
- Body image issues
- Poor social skills

- Lack of professional etiquette
- Knowing difference between personal life and professional life
- Lacks to gather audience connection

These are some of the core factors that need to get emphasized on. Focus to develop and project a desired image through grooming, clothing selection and in many cases training in etiquette and self-presentation. Good communication, knowledge of current trend in fashion, makeup and hair is must.

An individual who works with people to change, refine or enhance their appearance, behavior, communication or digital footprint, through variety of services, they start to utilize these concepts to image pull together and authentic and cohesive personal brand so to lead them-selves in the correct way.

The Power of Personal Branding is in three questions-

- Who you are?
- How you want others to perceive you?
- How others perceive you are?

Your personal brand and your image help you to identify and then communicate about what makes you unique and relevant and different to your targeted audience. Personal branding is the impression you leave on the hearts of people. To be authentic, transparent and consistent are the keys to improve you!

***

[7]
EXECUTIVE PRESENCE AND PEROSNAL BRANDING PRESENCE

"DRESS HOW YOU WANT TO BE ADDRESSED"

Introduction-

An image consultant strategically assesses some or all of the ABCDs of a client's image. It deals with appearance, behavior, communication and digital footprint. It is grooming plus hygiene. Dress for success, it helps to lift your morale and increases your self-esteem.

Appearance-

Appearance is an important factor and where we often start when looking at the overall image. You would think it is as simple as telling someone to wear this and not that, but there is so much more to this step. Color consulting, style that matches your current profession and your personality, fabric types and care, men's wear and suits, cost and your current closet, hair style and make up, board room attire and so much more all makeup the appearance that the client puts out into the world and uses to their advantages. Appearance highlights your uniqueness, likes, dislikes, tastes, flavors etc.

Behavior-

This is where image consulting starts to take on a much different thread than your typical wardrobe or personal stylist because it is beginning to shape and cultivate and an overall image and not just the one that shows up on the outside and is seen by all.

Behavior is just as important as your outside image because it brakes only surface what you put out into the world. Behavior is all about your attitude. Does your attitude reflect the position that you are in? Are you leading by example? Examining a client's current behavior and realigning them with the image that want to create and project is where the image consultant comes into play.

This leads us into the next step that any good image consultant will follow up with their client.

Communication-

It is another factor in making sure your client's image is in line with the position, they have now, but also the position they want to aspire to be in. One of the best things about communication is something that can be taught and learned and this is where any good communicator comes in.

Teaching communication skills is not easy as saying "Hey, just say it this way", you must get to know your client so you can effectively find ways to improve on the communication. Skills they already have and also help them find new ways to contribute and set themselves apart from the pack.

Digital footprint –

In the digital age we live in, many do not understand the importance of a footprint on the web that reflects and image they want to show to the world. One post, one comment, one share or one photo can damage reputation quickly. It is up to the image consultant to round out their client's overall image by hitting on this specific target. They can help their clients' review what currently is being seen online by others and how they can be sure what they are sharing and how they are sharing it is part of larger picture that is their image and often what others may be seeing before they even meet them in person. *"Google can be your friend or your worst enemy."*

***

[8]
PERSONAL GROOMING

Sometimes it becomes difficult to guess the type of style one possesses. Well, I am talking about the style which is trendy, dramatic, business formal, business casual, or mixture of all. Getting right details of you is very important in today's life race. Having reference to above;

Trendy- This style is for someone who follows current style and trends. They are innovative and understand street fashion.

Business casuals- This style includes comfortable, professional clothing with trouser pants, dressy jeans, buttoned downs and walking shorts.

Business formals- this is the classic, tailored, clean look in solid colors.

Dramatic- The style that is bold and theatricals. It makes a statement about someone who is not afraid to stand out and is comfortable wearing bold colors and prints.

So which style is yours? Are you mixture of all? If this is the situation you need to give some serious thought to your style. Because mixing different style will confuse people to know who you are.

Start to focus on your style and gather pictures from books or a magazine that perfects you and that represents you well. Personal style combines your file for your accessories, your shoes, handbags, haircuts or anything that appeals to you. Make sure everything works perfectly to create a cohesive statement.

You do not need to reinvent your wardrobe or invest in expensive clothing to enhance your style. Just follow below given tips to enhance personal style that works for you.

- Use color to make a statement-

  Managing a proper color statement for your clothes is something to get ourselves in a presentable manner. Fashion trends are changing day to day and keeping in touch with fashion is always good but in the same way accepting them would be excellent. Including that what calls to you inside that counts. After all you are going to be the one to wear colors. Just a pop of color makes everything look different. You should focus on colors that enhance your body and features. Lift tailored grey pants, lavender or rose color top and floral print scarf which is going to be optional would be a proper fit. Identify what colors call to you? Always have combination set of attire in your wardrobe; it will help you to be presentable, manageable and stress-free while choosing your color and style.

- Use black the right way-

  "Who loves black?" just kidding, everyone!! Black is mysterious one and dark which goes with every color. But not everyone looks good in black. In this case, you can use black as complimentary or make sure you put a more complimentary color next to your face with a scarf or necklace. Choose midnight black, blue, dark grey or chocolate brown instead of black for same style statement.

- Add fabrics and texture to create interest and make a statement-

  Fabric involves smoothness, smell, touch and sound. Think about sound of beads and cutting of cloth, touch of silk and satin on your skin. Using printed satin shirt inside a business jacket is something that creates special effect. Go through your drawers, your closet, your accessories and create a combination match for unique you.

- Use accessories to bring a correct "YOU"-

  Unique pieces will highlight your individuality and set you apart from all. Jewelry is something different and carries another special effect. Choice of belts, different watches that might be professional ones or casual ones, ties, necklaces for women, scarfs for both men and women, cuff bracelets in gold or silver with colored stones are going to showcase you with perfection. Start shopping and add a few high qualities, one-of-a-kind accessories into your wardrobe and don't forget to have an effective use out of it.

- Collection of investment piece that lasts for long time-

  Cheap chic hardly lasts beyond the season. Use garments and accessories to add current vibe to your image. Expensive ones would be expensive one for you but make sure you definitely purchase at-least one in each season so to have a great collection at the end.

- Attention to your best features-

  V-neck tops and U-shaped necklines lift your bust and focus the eye on your face. Add a necklace to make a statement. Paly with different necklines to see what works best for you.

Once you start focusing on these aspects after discovering what suits you the best, it will no longer be hard for you to play with different style statements and discover the new "YOU". Carry a list with you and focus and focus on the style you want to communicate when you shop for your clothing and accessories. Now, it's just time to enhance yourself and express a perfect one that describes you and your profession the best and an authentic one.

***

[9]
GETTING CORRECT DETAILS OF 'YOU'

Looking good is not enough! May it be your personal life or may it be your professional one, image or appearance is important, but one must also work on non-verbal messages they send to outside world. From body language to business and social etiquette- your behavior and communication skill play an important role in career. Your first impression should always be strong. If you are unable to strengthen your image, you will be most common image spoiler for the people you meet and greet. A deep insight into dress code levels and dress code policies will help you to determine the right wardrobe pieces.

Grooming-

Grooming is nothing but taking care of one's looks hygiene and clothing. It is to know about what to do and to put it into practice on a daily basis.

It starts before you put on your clothing. It means taking care of your physical self, hair, skin, face, hands and your total body. It helps to life your morale and increases your self-esteem.

What is hygiene?

Hygiene is a type of adopted practice. Have a bath every day your freshness should come across, rinse or wash your face at least two times a day. Brush your teeth and use mouthwash daily. Drink plenty of water to keep your insides clean. This will also help to keep your skin fresh on the outside.

Wear very little or no perfume, but in a country like ours, the use of a mild fragrance deodorant is compulsory.

Hands, Feet and Nails-

Your hand reveals about you. They should be clean and smooth. Nails should be clipped short and should be along the share of fingers. Your feet should be kept clean with no cracks. Delicate color gives sheen to nails.

Face-

Make it a daily habit to clean your face twice a day following cleansing, toning and moisturizing, one after the other. Use face wash for cleaning your face. It should be according to your face type. Toner is must to give precious moisture to the skin.

Make up-

Make up is essential but should be natural looking. The make-up should make you look fresh throughout the day. Bright colors in nail polish and lipstick should be avoided. Make up , if required can be refreshed during the day, but it should never be applied in public. Learn how to apply make up properly.

Hair-

Your hair should complement your face and complexion. Sport a maintainable length and style. If hair is longer than the jaw line, it should be tide or made into a bun. Hair holding devices should be in plain/ natural colors. Hair should be styled such that it is away an out of your face. Wash your hair at least two to three times in a week. And then do not forget to use conditioner shampoo, cleanses but also dries the hair. Oily, sticky and smelly hair in office is a no-no. Hair color should not be more than one or two shades darker or lighter than your natural hair color.

Health-

For the body to look attractive outside, it should be healthy inside. The right diet will keep you fit. One two outings a week, meditation, gym will keep you fit. Sleep well or be prepared for dark eye circles! Practice simple chair exercises if your work involve in front of computer for long duration, watch your pose.

Clothes-

Fashion and styling has always been the domain of women wear, while menswear has long been one of the neglected and more conservative areas. But for several years now, the growth of the men's fashion market has outpaced that of women wear. On the back of increasing demand, brands and designers are constantly expanding menswear lines also.

How you dress depends upon four factors:

The industry in which you work, the job you have within that industry the geographic area in which you live and what your client expect to see.

Look around you, what people are wearing and see if you don't make judgments about *'who they are!'* their line of business, their personalities and their competencies. Your choice of business apparel speaks to your professional behavior and creditability. It is important to understand, how to dress for business and outside world in your day to day life, if you wish to promote yourself and your organization in a positive manner.

***

[10]
CORPORATE GROOMING AND ETTIQUETTE

Most companies invest significant time, money and resources perfecting their corporate brand and image. Employees play a big part in how that corporate brand is delivered and defined inside and outside the company.

'DRESS FOR SUCCESS'

Considering your personal and professional life, 'The first impression you give when you enter a room is in the basic form of how you look' shall be considered. You need to realize that the way you dress and project yourselves and the color you wear are the initial form of communication and it is of utmost importance that you should make of your wardrobe colors and personal grooming.

Your work clothes should be viewed as an investment in your future. You should have the ability to visualize the correct mix of clothes, fabric, and style to make your image unique.

Professional dress for men

Choose a conservative suit in navy, black or grey either pinstripe or solid. The quality of material speaks as loudly as the color and can make a huge difference. A solid white or blue dressed shirt with long sleeves offers the most polished look. The more pattern and color you add, the more the focus on your clothing, rather than your professionalism. Ties should be made of silk, or silk like fabric. Avoid the cartoon characters and go for simple and subtle if you want to enhance your credibility. Socks should be calf length or above

Belts need to match or closely coordinate with your shoes. Once again, quality matters.

Keep jewelry to a minimum, in a time when men, sport gold necklaces, bracelets and earrings, the business professional should limit him to a conservative watch, a wedding band and may be his colleague ring.

Professional dress for women

The same overall rules apply to women's work attire as apply to men's. Business clothing is not reflection of the latest fashion trend.

Pants should brake at the top of the foot or shoe. Capri pants are out of place in the conservative business environment. When it comes to accessories less is once again more. Keep it simple: one ring per hand, one earring per year. Accessory should reflect your personality, not diminish your credibility.

***

[11]
SELF ANALYSIS

'SELF ANALYSIS ADDS STARS TO YOUR PERSONALITY, WORK, MANAGEMENT!'

SELF ANALYSIS

Self analysis is making analysis of you yourself in regard with your own personality, emotions, and behavior without help of any person. For imbuiltment of brand within you; have stress on three factors, you to be good at.

In order to grow & be successful, one must be able to know oneself. Self analysis is knowing yourself better. Your efficiency, your potentials, strengths and weaknesses all are revealed through self analysis. It helps an individual get closer to his or her personality and repair what needs to be amended in order to face success. For self assessment you should keep track of strengths and weaknesses which will help realise and guide you to work on what needs to be ammended or to be removed and develop talent and abilities within you. Consider your strength, weakness, opportunities and threats of individual or business ventures. Discover and appreciate the strengths within you, define the weaknesses so that you can minimise them, make out most of the opportunities that present you, recognise the possible threats and treat them in organised and planned way. Self analysis is the best analysis.

You should keep track of your strengths and weaknesses so often that it will help realize and guide you to work on what needs to be amended or permanently removed and will help to develop your own talent as well as your own ability.

Recognize your own strength and weaknesses and the opportunities and threats you face, or in a work context for analysing the strengths, weaknesses, opprtunities and threats a business or event faces. What you have to do is just follow the following-

- Always appreciate for what you are doing and what you are up with, it will help you to decide your strength.
- Make list of your weaknesses on which you have to work on and try to minimise them.
- Make way for the opportunities and be presentable and participable in them so that you can lead from others ahead in what you are with.
- Have a look on possible threats and treat them in organised way.

All the above points will definetly help you lead from others and the crowd you are standing with. This will help you add a extra star than others. You must identify yourself a 'BRAND' and keep addressing a different you.

'Be Realistic And Focused On What Really Happens ,
You Will Definetly Find a Way Out To Represent a Better You.'

***

[12]
EFFECTIVE COMMUNICATION

Communication is something that is linked with conversation. Every time you talk to stranger some sort of metal link is form or in easy language a sort of connection. Every conversation after that you have with them gets stronger. Think over it, how interesting it sounds that every day you start talking to stranger how many more contacts you would develop in a day, a week, a month or in a year. We all of us are aware of 'Humans Connect with Humans' so build new link and at the end you will have a massive world wide web. Communication opens door, it can make war and can make peace and conversation define who we are in the human race. Every single person in your life was a stranger to you, but communication made it easy to connect you with them.

Communication is such a factor in making sure you people create an image in line with the position you have now, but also the position you want to aspire to be in. Teaching communication skills is not as easy as saying "hey, just say it in this way" but you must get to know how important are the usage of words while having a conversation. Remember, your one word can be so influential to one and on other hand can also affect other.

It reflects an image that you want to show to the world. Your one word, one comment, one talk or resemblance can damage a reputation quickly.

May be you are any working individual whether working front-end or back-end, or an entrepreneur or single working women or an individual everyone reflects themselves through way of conversation. You must find new ways to contribute and set yourself apart from the pack.

Let's take communication like a concept written book manner; but in interesting sense-

Communication is one of the profound ways to change brain chemistry. As people begin to speak, their blood pressure goes up and microscopic blood vessels changes are detectable at far distant point in the body.

When people listen attentively or tune into the external environment in a relaxed manner, their blood pressure falls and heart rate slow down, often slightly below normal listening level.

Now onwards, keep this in mind and notice it whether it happens with you or not; well it happens it with all!

Effective communication is an essential component for success in any kind of sector you are working or non-working in, whether it is interpersonal, intergroup, organizational, or external level. In any communication, at least some of the meaning is lost in simple transmission of message from sender to the receiver. In many of the situations a lot of the true message is lost and the message that is heard is often far different than the one intended.

***

[13]
TALKING TO STRANGERS, WHY?

"Conversation Is Like Reading A Book, You Can Check Pour Out Any Chapter Of Life, Any Page You Want To And You Wish To Visit To!

DECIDE WHETHER- ***You Just Want To See Title Or Take A Book, Open The Page And Start Reading A Story."***

As you read earlier, conversation is something that creates link between people stronger and stronger. To connect to the outside world you need to have conversation as you meet strangers the grocery guy, driver, customers, clients, etc. While carrying any conversation; you need to break small talks; big conversations are waiting for you to know the unknown person. You get to know many things. Being a woman *how can I talk to anyone who I don't know?* It's totally wrong; be open. It's not like that women should feel afraid or uncomfortable and men should be open to have information from stranger. But one thing to remember for always, don't forget to have an eye contact while having conversation. It shows the way of your confidence. And by doing this soon you will begin to notice how words can change minds! Just because you have communication problem or are unable to stand up confidently at the places you are new at, you should rather wait and have an understanding of the problem so that you can make yourself comfortable till you get the chance to show your abilities and your ideas to carry an important conversation.

"YOU START SAYING……THEY WILL START THINKING"

This is nothing but the culture one adopts and others become frame dependent. One conversation with anyone makes yourself think and others around you also think.

Suppose, you are having any product to sale into the market. What will you do? You'll highlight your product to come up and you behind it! Human connects with humans and not with logos, and so you need to stand up to carry an influential conversation to convince one-another.

Remember, every person gives a summary of their personal communication style in terms of what they know is what works for them and others seem to comprise their uniqueness. Communication is the ability to relate to the people leading to inter-personal connection and ability to sort out conflicts or talks which are said to be the basics of a good communicator. So deal with nerves and structure a good communication style.

***

[14]
MEN AND WOMEN- WAY TOWARDS DEVELOPMENT AND THEIR STANCE

This corner is going to be something special for each and every person there with a sort of motivation and excellence. It is need of an hour for anyone of us whether men or women to make themselves stand in the world of competition.

'FREEDOM'

Most of the times, person need freedom from most of the eagerness to accept the mediocre, freedom to create an identity of her, freedom for her enjoyment, freedom to be expressive in terms of fashion, education, identity, creativeness, and many more different things. There seems the need to push for excellence in everything they aspire for.

Breathing free air is no longer enough. Everyone deserves freedom to live without any kind of apprehension and doubt. One word 'Freedom' defines open cherish-ness to one's life. How beautiful the feeling is, reading the word Freedom, isn't it! Immediately many things strikes to mind when one read the word Freedom which carries the unique beauty in it-self. One word that means a lot of things to a lot of people. Some value economic freedom, others count the freedom to choose as most important. For few, the freedom to express is paramount while many guard their freedom to be alone. Everyone have that one freedom that is being cherished the most- something that define 'YOU'!

Freedom is something that one can't live without. Let's try to define freedom-

- Freedom is something that allows pushing the body, mind and soul towards pure excellence.
- Freedom is something that don't let you live in the state of constant fear of being trolled, robbed, facing malice, etc.
- Freedom is something that comes naturally if you are always on the right path.
- Freedom is something that is generated for your loved ones, for those whom you care more or want to be with.
- Freedom is to be like a free bird that flies around without any restrictions and boundaries.
- Freedom is something where you can express your love, thoughts, feelings, care, worth, ability, responsibility, confidence and this list doesn't tells to stop; it continues, continues and continues.

You should remove all toxics and be yourself in such a way that you will become an example for others. Social life is extremely important because fitting in with the peers can make the difference between feeling confident and being one of those who struggles to fit in.

'Don't steal <u>Yourself</u> from the person known as YOU'

***

[15]
DRESS TO EXPRESS

"DRESS HOW YOU WANT TO BE ADDRESSED"

Everything that connects with you results in your inside- out and generates different emotional, physical and mental effects.

You can use colors to boost energy or to create calmness, to make people smile or to take them in notice. Different color communicates different level of power and energy to reflect about your intentions. Let's see what colors say and reveal.

- *Muted colors are touched with grey-*

  Muted colors are soft colors. It considers all shades of grey and lighter neutrals. Muted colors depict beauty, order, quality.

- *Saturated colors-*

  These colors combine warm colors and bright colors. Saturated colors depict life, love, and laughter. Wear these colors when your intention is to bring more enthusiasm, connection and warmth into your life.

- *Shaded colors touched with black-*

  When your intention is to bring more wisdom and sensitivity to life wear these colors. These colors are darkest colors like black, darkish blue, charcoal color and many other dark shades. These colors reveal your calmness, creativity and serenity.

- *Toasted colors-*

  These are browns, taupe, tans and beiges. Toasted colors reveal loyalty, security and stability. One should wear such colors when intention is to bring more tradition, commitment and support into life.

- *Tinted colors are touched with white-*

  They are fresh and clear tones. Wear these colors when your intention, is to bring more expansion, learning and motivation into your life.

  Getting right details about yourself is very important as it helps you to stand with unique identification. Dress to express is something that will lead you towards your goal and increase contact with the public. This will set you apart for creating and convincing yourself towards general public.

***

[16]
SIGNATURE STYLE

There is always one person in the crowd who captures absolute attention with their look. All eyes gather at the one when they scan the room and all focus is made on them. That person radiates his or her own signature style adorned with the items perfect match for them. Their signature style speaks of who they are because they dress with their own personal energies, intention and personal coloring in mind. You can be that man or woman.

Signature style is something that shows the *'who'* inside you. Your signature style creates your first impression to start with and last impression where you are going to end it.

'Signature Style Is Something That Positions People to Turn Head Towards You'

It's not all about purchasing clothes or shopping or spending money but it is the blend of your inner energy, dedication, personal intention towards who you are.

It is based on your fabric design that suits you and your personality; it is about customized colors and about stylistic look that you choose for yourself.

Let's take an example; suppose you are manufacturer and businessman and have invented a product to launch into the market. Yes, off course! Your product deals well and reaches to high positive effects to public. Now people want to know about 'who' invented the respective product?

Think over it, at that movement would you be able to present yourself confidently? Would you be able to carry yourself properly? Just sitting behind gadgets doesn't make others reveal about true you and your true personality! About, *'Who you are?'* Make sure, you represent yourself well and after that your respected product with you and not you behind your product.

Your signature style is your first expression of who you are to those you meet. When you think of signature style think of color, design, look, intent!

What colors suits you? What makes you feel confident? What turns you on and brightens enthusiasm from you and "fits" you more than all others.

Every time new trend arrives and every season speaks of different colors. Sometimes floral, sometimes bright, sometimes light. Color is the first thing you see and the last thing you forget. Right selection of color can make an outfit enhance your facial tone and transform your appearance. Color always seems to speak. They define your inner you reflecting your choice. They define you, your choice, your personal beauty, your deepest self. Color changes your mood. It is equally responsible to make you silent one or the vibrant one.

Just think of yourself as a blank canvas and clothing as a verbal art. Start filling positive statements and affirmations adorning you in the most enjoyable manner and fill your blank canvas with the proper judgment of colors that speaks about you.

You can incorporate color on three different levels and they are essence, intention and personal color.

Essence-

Essence is honoring who you truly are. It reveals your real nature and what you are in your heart. It brings out an authentic you.

Intention-

Intention is about where you are going, what you expect to bring into your life.

Personal color-

Personal color is about your appearance, what people 'see' on the outside. It combines your eye, skin, hair and blushes coloring.

Considering this make sure, you get fabrics matched with your color analysis and the one that suits you will reflect you and keep in series of sequence.

***

[17]
WHAT IS INDIA MODERN?

Is it a saree? Or fusion wear? It's a question that has stumped most. But the modern Indian silhouette is quite like the country it aims to embody- a sum of all its parts. In the great change happening in Indian fashion, 'Modern Indian" is the term that's often bandied about but has no real meaning.' There is no single silhouette that defines India, it is undefinable one. From your salwar to wearing Indian saree worn with a t-shirt, everything is fusion. Even modern Indian brides are independent and bold about their choices.

The modern Indian woman relates to the past, but with a modern twist. She knows the value of heritage handloom; it mixes it with international brands. She mixes her jadau with diamonds. Her makeup may be international but her kajal is Indian. Her perfumes may be jo Malone but she'll layer it with a dab of ittar.

Fashion and Combinations are never ending. It comes up with pair and fusion. India modern has to have a conscientious element to it, because slow fashion is need of the hour. Handlooms play a big part and experimenting with accessories would be any time acceptable.

For instance traditional saree can be draped more dramatically paired with an embellished belt and statement earrings. Wear a saree with leggings instead of a petticoat, and a sexy corset as a choli. Wear chunky wooden jewelry with your kanjeevaram silks, and sarees with oxford lace up shoes. Indian fashion covers wide range of clothing from ornate clothes designed for wedding ceremonies to pret lines, sports and casual wear. It even includes the traditional Indian techniques of embroidery like chikhen, crewel and zardosi. Sarees are woven in silk, cotton and artificial fibers. Paithani, Kanjivaram, Banarsi, Mysore, Bandhini are some varieties of beautiful sarees from different regions of India. In Rajasthan and Gujarat men wrap and twist a length of cloth in the form of dhoti around their lower limbs and a shirt like kurta. Colorful turbans complete the picture of Indian people. In urban India women generally wear Salwar Kameez and the Cudidaar Kameez, is worn by women who go to work and the saree is worn on formal occasions. Men wear kurta and pajamas, or a Sherwani for a formal wear. Western wear such as shirt are trouser are commonly worn by men across India. Jeans, t-shirt, capris, Bermuda are the kind of casual clothing worn by the young, who are said the trendsetters of fashion and fusion in India.

Indian clothing and its fair description is never ending. It gathers attention of everyone and the change, mixture and blends are mesmerizing one. The list of fashion and trend never ends. New arrives and the cycle continues with its never ending list.

Well with all this the right kind of accessories are also important with the type of fusion wear one adopts. Accessories are the item that sets you apart with a different and ever looking shine on your body.

***

[18]
REDEFINING ACCESSORIES

'YOU ARE ONLY LIMITATION ON PUTTING TOGETHER THE PERFECT OUTFIT IN YOUR IMAGINATION'

Accessories are the one that adds-up your value; each and every minute detail of using accessories is worth describing yourself. Thus, don't limit your perfect outfit by not wearing accessories.

Let's get one task done, imagine you have to get presented at fashion game ,where you have to make arrangement of accessories on the given outfits say-

- Dark wash straight jeans with a basic white t-shirt.
- A little black dress with a matching jacket.

Now, your goal is to come up with the most diverse, innovative and attractive outfit possible, using just accessories added to your two basics above.

While doing this, you will-

- Have a much better idea of what 'must- have multitasking, go anywhere' accessories are.

- Know what accessories you currently own and are overlooking and can now organize and interchange them.
- Discover what missing essentials you need to add to your existing wardrobe inventory.
- Realize you are much more creative than you ever thought possible.

The above activity will get easy for you to perform and match up with, after having a look at proper accessory detailing.

As an added bonus, accessories are absolutely your best friend on any trip. They enable you to come up with any number of dynamite looks to fit any business or social obligation. If you don't think so, just watch how interesting will it be to express yourself.

- Remember, accessorizing should be selected and done by keeping your own personal brand in mind. All your accessories should be an extension and expression of your personality.
- For example, dramatic and bold accessories, such as bright, shiny, angular pieces in black or red would look completely out of place on a small, curly-haired with romantic personality; that time you should be wearing delicate antique jewelry.

While browsing to season's fashion trend, don't just accept or follow it blindly. The right kind will only give right information about you.

ACCESSORISING MEN

A lot of men have different opinions about wearing accessories. They think it's too jazzy for their work profile whereas some of them think it's not just necessary. But it might help you to reconsider it in a better way for work, for fun or just because world needs more sharp men. It is very important to know that today people look for details in an overall outfit rather than just a generic effort towards your dressing style.

TIE-BAR

Every man possesses at least one tie in his collection. Let's see what details it gives.

- A slim straight body should have narrow or slim tie.
- A Wide torse or huge belly should go for a wider tie.
- With a plain shirt contrast one or one with pattern will suit well.
- On check shirt, wear a plain single color tie and select tie type that matches any one color from the check pattern.
- Now talking at tie bars, everyone knows what tie bars is, but have never bothered to understand the need of having one. Tie- bar is also a tool that keeps your tie in place and is used to stick your shirt.

Tie-bar

Tie-bar

Occasion to wear-

Wedding, corporate meeting, business meet, gala dinner.

Tips-

- Be careful at bar not clipped too hard that it crushes your shirt and tie.
- Wear your personal tie and choose an appropriate tie-bar.
- Tie bar should be perpendicular to your tie.
- Never wear tie bar while wearing waistcoat.
- Select good quality tie-bar.

COLLAR BAR

Collar bar or collar pin are the most dapper looking accessory in a man's wardrobe. It is used to hold the tips of collar in a dress (usually in formals) shirt together so that the knot of the neck tie just out appropriately. This is going to keep fine with the minute details you want to give outside and assures that you are distinctly different than the mediocre ones.

Like the previous accessory, there are few things you need to understand about collar bar.

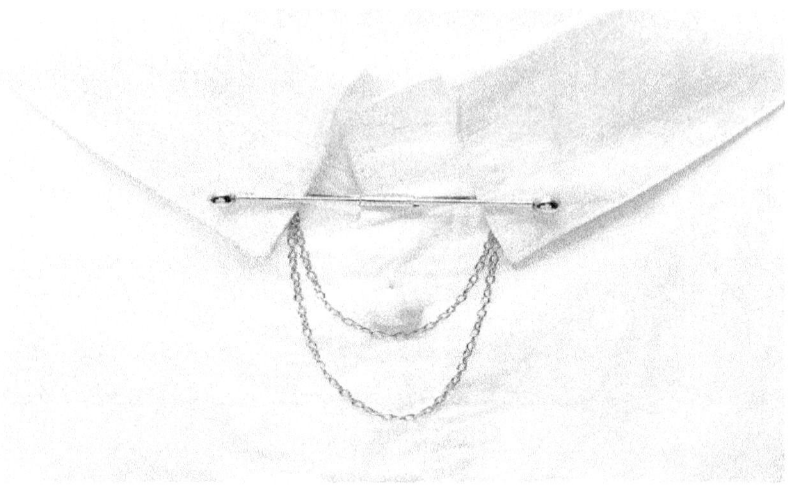

Collar bar

Occasions to wear-

Office wear, award ceremony, business meet.

Tips –

- Make sure the quality is of best standard.
- Use collar bars only with tailored shirts as they would give you perfect eye-lets for the bar and are specially designed for tailored shirts.
- If you are wearing on a ready-made shirt make sure the collar is not stiff and fabric is soft, this will save you from creating whole to your collar and will not give shabby look.
- White collared shirt will amplify collar bar at its best.

MEN'S RING

Men's ring

Class rings, wedding rings and championship rings from any sport event are all significant one and to be worn with pride in a situation where formal clothes are called for. Other than that usually only wedding ring is worn.

WOMEN ACCESSORSING

Now further let's take a glimpse at accessories that are defined for girls. Its all-round accepted that accessories are girl's best friend and no specific to define about. Girl's accessories put a large variety and a well-structured combination and type can go with perfect combination of set of clothes worn. Still have something in detail for you below.

Everyone wants to make a good first impression, so make sure these invaluable staples are in excellent condition and the best quality you can afford.

- A good quality of heels; dress them up or down with jeans, a dress or a suit.
- One good quality of purse.
- A good quality watch, the best you can afford.

OTHER INDISPENSABLE

- A pashmina that every women should have. Collection of pashmina with different colors will take you anywhere, anyplace as a cover up, a winter scarf or just for warmth.

Pashmina

- A large everyday purse.
- A neutral, evening purse.
- A pair of metallic sandals.
- Designer sunglasses.
- One good belt that fits through pants loops or may be worn on its own.

TRENDY SEASONAL PURCHASES TO UPDATE YOUR WARDROBE

- Sleeveless top depending on season's colors.
- Shoes as per trend.
- A scarf in hot new color.
- A piece of customized jewelry that suits your personality and helps updating your look.

Now you are all set to change things up with accessories, start rejuvenate and reinvent your wardrobe. Come up with new and varied combinations and be creative while making you well dressed up.

***

[19]
FREEDOM FROM FASHION RULES

<u>'THERE'S NOTHING LIKE- FOR A BODY TYPE, FEEL FREE TO WEAR'</u>

A lot of people consults image consultant for styling advice. They usually have queries about what to wear with a particular body type or for occasion or pairings. Well, there are no clear answers to such style dilemmas because you are living in an era where none of the old rules exist or apply. Fashion is not just giving trend that people are coping; it's a means of self-expression. It's an identity. You can wear clashing prints, or sneakers with a formal dress, pair a shirt with lehenga. This time is the one when trends are co-existing- you just pick and choose what you want to wear. Just the important one is to remember is –

"The Big Freedom Today Is To Wear Whatever You Want but Carry It with Confidence and Conviction Rolled Up in Your Sleeves"

Always wear the things that make you feel confident, empowered and comfortable. Fashion is more than just an industry that comes up with newer trends, outfits and pieces of clothing. The age old rules no longer apply. The whole point of being fashionable and stylish is to understand that there are really no rules. Picking out an outfit should be fun, enjoyable experience. 'I try my best to experiment because I love to and not because that is the norm. Fashion is not just about wearing the clothes that look amazing, but also about creativity, experimentation and breaking the norm. The acceptance has increased; especially, in the cities, you can see boldness and nonchalant attitude people have when it comes to their style. Well you have to accept that social media plays a huge part in really exposing people to trends around the world.

Some of you reading might be thinking, all this reading could be acceptable but, what about fat girls? Can fat girls do fashion?

Let me tell you, yes of course! Fashion has become freer. People think it will be a wired one when fat girls want to be fashion freak. But, leave everything back and be a fashion influencer. Yes, norms do exist and especially for marginalized bodies but a lot has been broken too. You need confidence to do what you want to do. There are still a lot of no-no's like 'body types', color blocking and 'you can't wear a crop top' – especially for plus- sized bodies. But you break them by asking one simple question: why the hell not me?

Talking at different body shapes: do you know what's your body shape? Yes, it could be interesting to know what body shapes you posses with the reference to further topics.

Fashion is more democratic now. With so much of content to consume at every second and so many ideas via celebrities and real life influencers, fashion is within everyone's reach. Breaking the stereotypical view of how men and women should ideally dress, you have now become open to experiment. The biggest anti-fashion rule that has become the highlight is anti-fit clothing which is for all body shapes and types. Another major shift is from fast fashion to slow fashion. Trends crop up, styles change and rules are broken every day. But at the end of the day, do what makes you happy. Break stereotypes and open your boxes of wishes. The critique of fast fashion is to pile it high, sell it cheap and hang the consequences. Also with all this it is also important to get notice while accepting fashion is what the environment needs for getting an appropriate message through fashion trends.

***

[20]
DEFINING WOMEN BODY SHAPE

Every woman has a different and unique body shape which is manageable one. Rather than fighting with, learn to live with it and love your body.

Many times one have unsuccessful shopping trips only because of the fact that you think nothing will fit correctly or look good. If so is the situation, you are like many other women who suffer from insecurity and are not able to adjust with your body flaws.

But, you could be able to manage it if you can change the silhouette of your body, create or show-off curves, look slimmer, play with your assets and move the focus away from trouble areas by wearing correctly fitted clothes.

Most of the stylish women also don't possess a perfect body shape but are able to manage by focusing on what to wear and what to avoid. They choose clothes that accentuate their perfect areas and minimize their less than perfect areas.

Once you start determining your body shape, you will start purchasing the costume that perfects you and you will automatically develop a sense of confidence letting fears and anxiety away.

There are four different universal body types:

- Diamond shape
- Hour-glass shape
- Pear shape
- Rectangular shape

Let's see what is your body type and what kind of costume you should dwell with and what should you avoid.

- DIAMOND SHAPE

In this case, your shoulders or bust are larger than your hips. Diamond shaped body has broad shoulders, a large bust and upper back, a narrowing at the waist and hips and slender legs.

If you have a diamond shape, dress to draw attention to the bottom half of your body and create an illusion of balance by accentuating your smaller hips and legs.

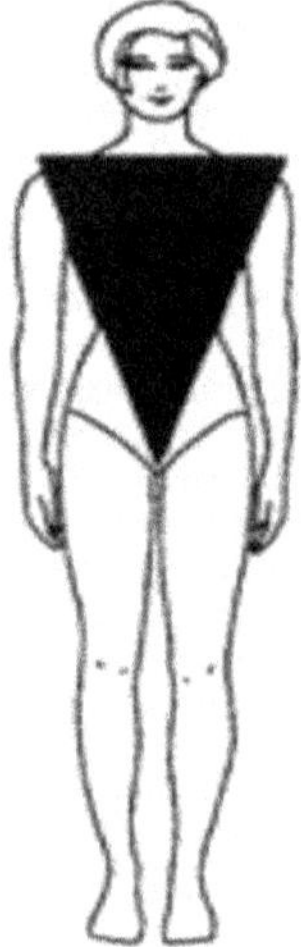

Figure of Diamond Shape Body Structure

TO WEAR

Wear the following to enhance your appearance and give a figure flattering silhouette-

1. V-necks and wrap tops that draw attention away from wide shoulders.
2. Tunics and flared or fitted tops that offer a soft, skimming definition and pull the eye to center of the body.
3. Shirts with straight look and little or no details.
4. Larger-strapped tank tops with a deep neck or V-neck that balance the lower body.
5. Jackets that flare at the waist and add volume.
6. Wide-legged, flared or boot-cut pants that balance out the larger upper half of the body.
7. Skirts and dresses with a bit of shape and wide hemlines such as A-line, softly pleated or tulip hemlines that draw attention to your shapely legs.

AVOID WEARING

1. Shoulder pads.
2. Skinny jeans or leggings that accentuate slim legs.
3. Tube tops, tops with thin straps or puffed sleeves, strapless tops, turtle-necks and crewnecks, since they draw attention to your wide shoulders.

- HOUR-GLASS SHAPE

Your shoulders and hips are about the same size and you have a very defined waist. The hour-glass shaped body generally has shoulders and hips that are similar in size and a defined waistline. Your aim is to embrace and maintained a balance silhouette.

Figure of Hour-Glass Shape Body Structure

TO WEAR

Wear the following to enhance your appearance and give a figure flattering silhouette-

1. Wear fitted-shift and belted shirtdresses that follow the lines of your body.
2. Wear fitted shirts that hug your curves.
3. V-neck and scoop-neck fitted tops that reveal a hint of cleavage and draw the eye-up to your chest.
4. Wear trench-style, belted coats.
5. Mid-rise pants, such as boot-cut or slightly flared styles, that minimize your hips and balance your body.
6. A-line, wrap and pencil skirts with the hem at or just above your knee to show off your legs.
7. Soft fabrics that drape and skim the body.

AVOID WEARING

1. Fabrics that add bulk to your body hide your curves.
2. Crop tops and loose, baggy peasant tops that hide the body.
3. Empire dresses and loose-fitting dresses that disguise your defined waist.
4. Low-rise jeans that make you look heavier.

5. Bell-shaped, box and pleated skirts that add volume to your hips.
6. Over-sized jackets that hide your body's shape.

- PEAR SHAPE

Your hips are wider than your shoulders. The pear shape body generally has hips and thighs that are wider than the shoulders or bust. This shape has several exciting features like sexy hips, a shapely bottom and a slime waistline. Aim at widening shoulder line, place the focus on the upper body and minimize the lower body in order to visually restore the balance.

Figure of Pear Shape Body Structure

TO WEAR

Wear the following to enhance your appearance and give a figure flattering silhouette-

1. Bright or lighter colors with texture and patterns on top to broaden the shoulders, bust and upper torso.
2. Dark colors on the bottom that add a slimming effect.
3. Necklines such as boat, scoop and V-necks that create a broader shoulder and reveal a narrow mid-section.

4. Empire, strap less, wraps and off-shoulder dress that help balance the body shape.
5. Fabric such as light knits and matte jersey that accentuate and smooth out the curves.
6. Shirts with small shoulder pads or breast pockets that add volume.
7. Pants with little or no waistband that flare slightly or have ease through the legs, and straight-leg or boot-cut jeans, wear at the natural waist or little lower.
8. Skirts that drape over the hips, such A-line, wrap or fit and flare; wear just below the knee.
9. Monochromatic mix-and-match separates that help create a balanced elongated look.
10. Accessories that draw the eye upward.

AVOID WEARING

1. Pleats, side pockets and details on backside pockets.
2. Circle, bias-cut and pleated skirts that add unnecessary volume to your hips.
3. Drop-waist or tunic styles that hide the waistline and cover the backside.
4. Pants with narrow or trapped legs.

- RECTANGULAR SHAPE

Your shoulders, bust and hips are similar in size and your waistline is undefined. A variation on this shape is oval, where the waist is slightly larger than the other measurements. The rectangle shaped body generally has shoulders, bust, waist and hips that are equal in size. You have a 'boyish' style figure since your body is straight up and down. Your aim is to define your waist. Have Aim of widening shoulders and adding curves to your hips to provide the illusion of an hourglass silhouette.

Figure of Rectangular Shape Body Structure

TO WEAR

Wear the following to enhance your appearance and give a figure flattering silhouette-

1. Tops with details around the hip and corset tops that give your body shape.
2. Shoulder pads, tops with V-necks and U-necks and wrap tops that flatter and create a curvy figure.
3. Jackets with structure or that cinch at the waistline to add curves.
4. Belted jackets like a trench that help create an hourglass silhouette.
5. Boot-cut jeans with a dropped waistline that adds some curves.
6. A-line, flared, circle and wrapped skirts that have waistlines and taper outward to create curves.
7. Accessories that draw the eye upward.

AVOID WEARING

1. Patterns with vertical lines.
2. Loose garments that add to rectangle shape.
3. Clingy fabrics that emphasize your boxy figure.
4. Pencil skirts without a waistband, especially ankle length skirts.
5. Long, straight-cut and double breasted coats that square off the body shape.
6. Wide or straight-legged pants that accentuate your body shape.

***

[21]
DEFINING MEN'S BODY SHAPE

<u>'FIND A MENTOR WITH WHOM YOU CAN DISCUSS AND FIND OUT SOLUTIONS FOR AREAS YOU SHOULD WORK ON AND YOUR STRENGTHS'</u>

It's important now to understand the time where not only women has to be kind of fit in all the areas of highlighting but in presenting fit in overall image to get set in today's workaholic world men are also given the importance.

There are rules that are always to be kept in mind while dealing with the image that is always an important factor to be stressed upon. This will not only make you stand but will give you results to lead in your daily as well as your professional life.

- *#rule 1*- Your body type should always take preference over fashion trends.
- *#rule 2*- Dress for the body you possess now. Don't put off wardrobe improvements for that two year diet plan you have been working on.
- *#rule 3*- Learn to emphasize the best aspect of your build and divert attention away from your undesirable features.

Now let's have a look what your body shape has to say about 'YOU'-

- RECTANGLE SHAPE

Men with rectangular body shape has tall and thin frame. Their shoulders are roughly the same width as their waist and hips.

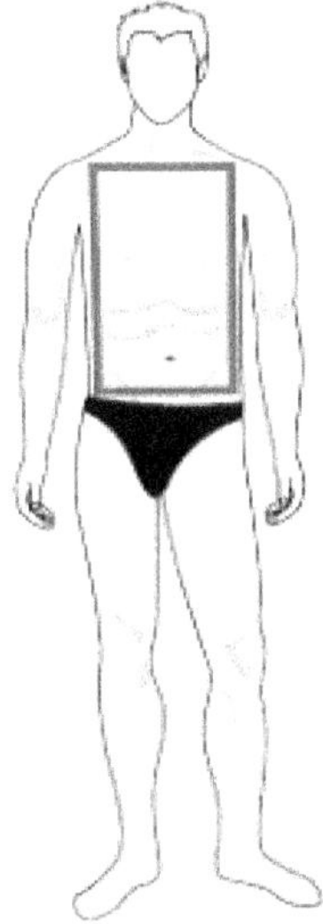

Figure of Rectangular Body Structure

TO WEAR

You should use clothing to widen your shoulders and add the effect of a subtle taper from your top down. You'll need to create an illusion of structure.

Wear the following to enhance your appearance and give a figure flattering silhouette-

1. Horizontal stripes-

Especially across your upper torso (short or long sleeved Breton tees), as they will add width to your slight frame.

2. Structured tailoring-

Once you have found structured blazers and suit jackets that add size to your shoulders, have your tailor take them in slightly at the back to emphasize your waist.

3. Layered looks-

A button down shirt and fine-gauge crew neck jumper is a no fail pairing that will add instant bulk to your frame.

4. Scarves-

A neatly tied or draped scarf is an easy way to add a point of difference to your look.

5. Prints, color pops and detailing-

Pops of brighter color up top or details like epaulets expand the dimensions of your otherwise slim frame.

AVOID WEARING-

1. Double breasted jackets-

Tailoring cut does not give much change or no change to rectangle shaped body. Go for single- breasted style where you can have plenty of structure in the shoulders instead.

- TRAPEZOID SHAPE

Such types of body shape are proportioned individuals with medium to narrow waist and hips and a broad shoulder and chest. The upper torso is usually larger than the lower torso.

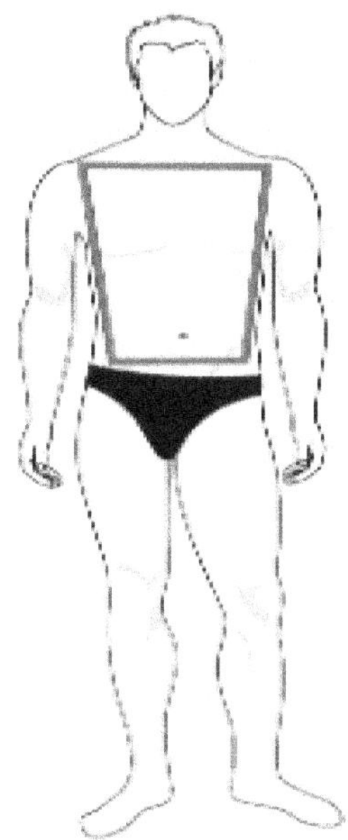

Figure of trapezoid body structure

TO WEAR

Make sure in trapezoid body shape you showcase your athletic body shape in slim and fitted clothes. Take advantage of sports inspired modern look for enhancement.

Wear the following to enhance your appearance and give a figure flattering silhouette-

1. Trousers-

Find your brand that close fit and have your trousers tailored. Most of the colors and patterns close fit your body line. Avoid baggy clothes.

2. Shirts-

Vertical strips will make your appear little taller. Checks and plaids add horizontal bulk so accordingly pick the one that suits your height.

3. Jackets-

A blazer or suit jackets tapers your waist, making your stomach seem slimmer and your shoulders seem broader. Wear it buttoned with a single button at waist for maximum effect.

4. Neckties-

Stick to normal length and normal width ties(about 3 to 3 ½).

AVOID WEARING-

1. The biggest no and no's to avoid wearing loose and saggy one.

- TRIANGLE SHAPE

Larger around the waist and hips in relation to the top part of their bodies consist of triangle body shape.

Having a triangular body shape does not mean that your are having bad shape but finds challenging while while finding clothes that suits your body line and make you appear proportional.

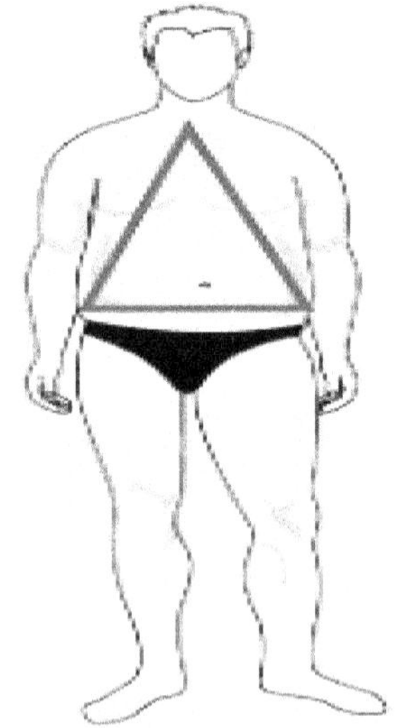

Figure of triangle body structure

TO WEAR

Try to create balance and shape with your clothes is key consideration for you.

Wear the following to enhance your appearance and give a figure flattering silhouette-

1. Tailored pattern blazers-

Wear checked blazers and fitted waist coats with solid trousers. The mix of print and solid colors will create the illusion of shape and take the focus away from larger waist.

2. Vertical strips-

This pattern creates a streamlined effect that elongates and slims down the upper body. Horizontal stripes are preferred only if they are visible from the chest upward.

3. Jackets with structured shoulders-

Slouchy shoulders on jackets will exaggerate your already sloping shoulder line.

4. Single breasted shoes-

Double breasted jackets add bulk to your waist. Single breasted jackets allow for a more relaxed and slimming fit. Get your jackets tailored for a structured fit on the top but with extra room around the waist.

5. Brighter color panels-

Patterns and detailing across the chest and shoulders help to broaden the upper torso. Wear jumpers and crew neck tees with color panels across the chest but a slimming darker color like grey, navy or black around the mid-section.

AVOID WEARING-

1. Fitted polo shirts and roll necks-

Both these styles tend to make the neck and shoulders appear slender while accentuating any roundness in the waist.

2. Brighter colors and busy prints-

Bold and bright patterns will draw attention to your triangular shaped torso. Work them into your outfit as accents in the form of pocket squares, glasses, socks. Bold belts will only draw attention to your width of your waist.

3. Skinny fits and extreme tapers-

Narrowing trousers draw the eye of an observer to the center of your body. Swap them for wide and straight leg fits that add proportion to your silhouette.

INVERTED TRIANGLE SHAPE

The shape of this body type is a big triangle with the base at the shoulders and the point at belly button. Your well-developed chest and shoulders are significantly broader in comparison to your waist and hips (probably this is the result of spending hours at gym every week working up an enviable muscle pump) and all this result in accentuated shoulders and thighs and a narrow waist.

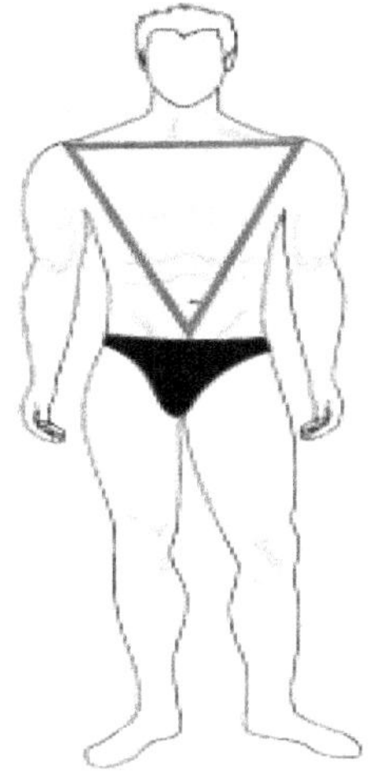

Figure of inverted triangle body structure

TO WEAR

Focus on lower body while balancing the proportions of your well-developed upper body. Wear close fitting clothes that reduce visual clutter and emphasize on sharp lines of your torso.

Wear the following to enhance your appearance and give a figure flattering silhouette-

1. Horizontal stripes-

Espccially from the chest down, to broaden your comparatively narrow waist.

2. Slim fit shirts-

You can wear shirts to show off your fit body but don't forget to size up.

3. Slim cotton polo shirt-

With a spandex mix will allow stretch across a broad set of shoulders and chest while creating a tailored look around the waist.

4. Regular V-neck t-shirts-

The collar shape has a narrowing influence on your chest and draws the eye down and away from the broadest part of the torso. Stay away from plunging V-neck t-shirts.

5. Straight leg trousers and jeans-

Slim fit pant will finely work for you whereas skinny jeans will accentuate your legs. Wearing patterned pants, camo shorts or checked trousers distracts from your upper body.

6. Trouser with larger seat drop –

Look for the trouser with larger drop measurement between the waistbands and the crotch seam.

7. Jackets-

Slim fit jackets that follow the natural line of your silhouette, with a bigger difference between the width of the torso and waist will suit you at best.

AVOID WEARING-

1. Structured tailoring-

Unstructured silhouette work better in streamlining your line rather than structured one.

- OVAL SHAPE

In such body shape the center of the torso is wider than the shoulders and hips. The rest of the build tends to reflect short.

Keep it simple and dark with a round body. Dark solid colors are always good.

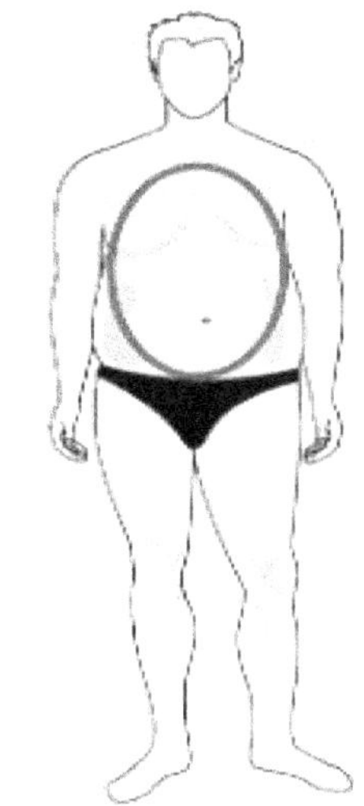

Figure of oval body structure

TO WEAR

Wear the following to enhance your appearance and give a figure flattering silhouette-

1. Trousers-

The trousers waist should be comfortable and loose. Never belt it tight so that it pinches and wrinkles.

2. Suspenders-

Wear suspenders as they hold the trouser front out slightly, letting it fall in a smooth front all the way past the crotch. Whether belted or worn with suspenders, the trousers should always be worn at the natural waist, where they can drape smoothly over the bottom of your stomach instead of squeezing it all upward.

3. Pleats-

Pleats will help pants widen slightly when you sit, adding a bit comfort for men with large thighs and bottoms.

4. Shirts-

A good fit is crucial in avoiding wrinkles that add up more bulk. Find a brand that work for you or else have your shirts tailored. A wider collar spread works well for broad men, especially when the neck and face are broad as well.

5. Jackets-

Dark, single breasted and only slightly tapered are keys to a good jackets for big men. A sharp taper at the waist is going to be hard to button and will stretch over the stomach.

6. Neckties-

Bow ties are best way to avoid a tie that drapes over the bulge of the stomach. If you are not comfortable with bow ties then go for decently wide and long ties that reach the belt.

AVOID WEARING-

1. Patterns and visual clutter is bad idea-

Generally patterns draw attention to mid area, and in such body structure we usually make viewers pay attention off the mid sections. Work on outfits that guide the eye smoothly up the whole length of the body and focus attention on your face.

2. Tight fits in the torso are bad choice-

Trying to fit in the clothing that is too tight is worst as it emphasizes the body's bulk and makes you look desperate.

At the end will suggest that you should try to identify the body structure and generate the change within you. It will surely work for you as you are the one who have secrets to look perfect.

***

COMPANION

Though you are of any age or any generation, this book will strengthen your important roots that are needed to generate the right kind of change needed. Most of the people neglect these important areas presented before you through this book or most of them are unaware of the same. Remember, first impression always pays you with good results and thus core areas cannot be neglected.

"CARRY THIS BOOK AS YOUR COMPANION, THIS WILL CERTAINLY PAY YOU WITH BEST RESULTS"

***

MAKE IT HAPPEN

"THOUSANDS OF THINGS SAID,

REMAINING SOME UNSAID...

THOUSANDS OF COLORS LIVED,

REMAINING SOME BEHIND...

THOUSANDS OF DREAMS ALIVE,

REMAINING YET TO GO THROUGH...

HEY YOU!!

WHAT WAITING FOR??

MAKE WAY FOR THEM

TO MAKE THEM HAPPEN.

Shivani Gohil

www.ingramcontent.com/pod-product-compliance
Lightning Source LLC
LaVergne TN
LVHW010457160826
845677LV00012B/2531

* 9 7 8 9 3 8 8 3 9 3 4 0 9 *